HEAT

AN INTERVIEW

WITH

JEAN SEBERG

HEAT

AN INTERVIEW
WITH
JEAN SEBERG

STEPHANIE DICKINSON

NEW MICHIGAN PRESS
TUCSON, ARIZONA

NEW MICHIGAN PRESS

DEPT OF ENGLISH, P. O. BOX 210067

UNIVERSITY OF ARIZONA

TUCSON, AZ 85721-0067

<http://newmichiganpress.com/nmp>

Orders and queries to nmp@thediagram.com.

ISBN 978-1-934832-41-9. FIRST PRINTING.

Printed in the United States of America.

Design by Ander Monson.

Cover art: "Saint Jean," oil on canvas, 16x20, by Jill
Hoffman.

CONTENTS

"She was the last generation
of the All-American girl and she went
farther than any of the others."

—Jean-Pierre Rassam

※ ※

[Seventeen-year-old Jean Seberg was chosen by Otto Preminger out of 18,000 fledgling actresses to star in his film *Saint Joan*. A girl from Marshalltown, Iowa, she became an instant celebrity and went on to star in *Bonjour Tristesse*, *Breathless*, *Lilith*, and *Paint Your Wagon*. She committed suicide at the age of forty in Paris, after having made 30 mostly European films. "She was one of the most appealing and enigmatic movie stars of the 1960s," said film critic Vincent Canby.]

SEBERG: MIDWEST NAIFF

Q: Iowa is an unlikely place for a celebrity to come from. While Marilyn Monroe is considered a mythic Los Angeles symbol, you're the Midwest's Muse. Tell us about the town that borders the Bible belt where you were raised.

SEBERG: Every place seems as unlikely as the next. You can't escape Marshalltown was the unsaid caution. When you swim in the forbidden sandpits the hydra growth invades and the town watches your white foot ease into hundreds of mouths. Marshalltown had the landlocked foursquare light of smoldering hymnals. It shone from the red maples and elms, the green dripping emeralds from branches. I left the town trees. Family. I eloped from tractor chug and roads of nowhere to go. Everything was thirst. Everyone knows your nightgown's color when you arrive in the funeral parlor.

You want Marshalltown. I buried my daughter there. Go find the graves of my parents and brother, and you'll see she's with them. Nina. I flew her from Paris in a glass coffin. Trinket-thing. Mourning doves nest and ditch lilies spring from her. Orange petals that shiver from human touch.

Night swims.

The waning town drowses.

I've drunk myself sober on darkness.

Each year on the anniversary of my baby's stillbirth

I attempt suicide. Have I any flesh left? Seven months pregnant I swallowed barbiturates thinking we'd both die, but then I survived.

*Q: Having lived in Iowa, I know there's no shortage
of pretty girls, but few ever claimed an international
reputation. Like many others, I wonder if you had been
only half as beautiful would you have married, raised
children, and been a housewife and not an actress?*

SEBERG: I don't claim anything not even a pretty face.
The Iowa River schooled me, although I was already
bigger than the place I'm from. At age four, my father
brought me here to watch bluegill and carp bite the
hook's surprise. The rocks oozed heat. Bass trees hung
heavily with vines and the current tugged the chocolate
sludge. In water they fought the line but once on
land, the knife glinting its cornsilk light, they gave up.
Where can we swim? Their wide-open sun-scalded eyes
began to die. I clenched my fists. *Throw them back!* The
fisherman laughed and cut. Slit open, the bluegill's petal
lungs still pumped. Tiny, translucent clouds of river
weather. At sixteen, I lived and breathed for *Photoplay*,
and you couldn't drag me to the cast and reel. The sneer
on Marlon Brando's lip I'd trace. Half as beautiful I
wouldn't have known the Hell that comes from having
a public. Fans. Or that I'd live Brando's words, "Success
on the screen usually means failure as a human being." If
someone had offered my mother pink Saturn ringed by
mysterious meteors and moons, she'd still have chosen
to make four babies and set the dinner table. Half as
beautiful, a quarter as beautiful, I'd still not settle for

housewifery in Marshalltown's green corn desert. I was always drawn to metamorphosis. The four stages of a butterfly. From egg to pupa to chrysalis to flight. I supped the flowers of a six-week life.

Q: You've been termed a naïf, a cross between the naïve and the waif, with a self-destructive bent. "I can do it by my 'lone" was said to be your first sentence. When your mother would tell you as a teen to clean your room, you'd reportedly answer: "I don't have to learn that. I'll be a movie star and have a maid to do my work." Could you comment on that?

SEBERG: I learned what I needed to. Because the heroes of movies at the Odeon Theatre smoked cigarettes I started to burn my fingers, striking matches with my thumbnail. I watched myself exhale, smoke curling its grey mystique over my face. James Dean muttered and puffed from the side of his mouth like a tormented saint. His cigarette hung from his lower lip and talked more than he did. From him I learned the shoulder-scrunch. Maybe I was the first actress who returned the hard stare of the camera. I was known for the blank look. The empty actress. Magnificent neck. Masochistic. Listen. A Midwestern girl is a good girl. She does as she's told. She's a drum majorette playing Sabrina in a high school production. A cluster of assigned meanings, not a biological being. She gives more than she takes. A virgin who believes all roads lead to white steeples. Like the red cardinal fish that swims in the deep sea with a lamp in its throat, she casts a glow. If she's able to act in four languages she'd better not claim to be smart or witty. I loved to shock. I married three times. My second husband, only a year younger than my father, was all bottle rockets and jigger chasers, black widows and exploding flame balls. He directed me in the worst film ever made. Before my shipwreck I was belting down pills, tumbling over the falls into the white water. I learned the meaning of the word venal. Insouciant. I darted before the camera like a minnow. Thin and stilted, said the critics. Unlike the Viking girl tied to the ship's prow by hanks of her hair, I was the rosebud stitched to a black brassiere. A gamine. My acting style derided.

Q: After Breathless, *shot on a $90,000 budget with a hand-held camera, Jean Seberg was a European brand. "La coupe Seberg," the boy-cropped hair, the Seberg trademark. How close to the real Jean is the free spirit Patricia Franchini, who sells the* Herald Tribune *on the Champs Elysées and takes up with a charming sociopathic killer?*

SEBERG: I walk in through the revolving door with no idea that I'll never find my way out. I confuse the masculine and feminine genders. Filmed in the Hotel du Suede on the Left Bank, the *Breathless* cameraman discovered even with my imperfect skin I had rare gifts: I was photogenic and an American girl who could speak French. In the heartland what's for sale is more concrete: a Hampshire fall boar, a porch swing, an abattoir. But who are you? A neophyte trailing behind the footlights. The sweet girl from Marshalltown before she becomes a monster. Jean, the tarte tatin, on the cover of *Réalités*. Pout, yes, part your lips. They're not skin at all but the plushest velvet recital dress. Wildflowers over thawing furrows. Lips worth $12,000 in mid-20th century dollars. Unlike co-star Jean-Paul Belmondo's eyes— deep skies with laugh lines nicked around them—the windows of my soul look about to drink cocoa. Under sheets, Belmondo and I ad-lib an all-afternoon love scene fully clothed. A chestnut horse clops by carrying Madame Bovary to her lover. Silly, repressed wench. I'll never die and that's what this fame means. Everything's a heartbeat. Your name: a hushing sound that even traffic can't drown. It's just teddy-bear-hugging under sheets. How impossible that far off suicide day in horrorland seems. Surely, it's not my fate.

SEBERG: STRANGLER OF SLEEPING MEN

Q: You've been trying to unbury the Midwest inside
yourself, so describe some drama from the dullest place on
Earth. What sparked the fanciful in you, the fever to act?
Speech class, movie magazines? Your father was druggist
and your mother, a teacher. Were any of your antecedents
artistic?

SEBERG: I had a terrible hunger for the theatrical.
Sundays we'd eat at my great-aunt's. My great-uncle Bill
sat in long-sleeved shirts three layers deep, hunched on
the Queen Anne's chair. He taught me to break the rule
of gaze. It's not the window behind him you crave or the
fence twined through with raspberries and wild grape,
but all the wildness cloaked under a shawl of dust. He'd
tell you naked women were climbing his red oak, the
same ones who slept in the chicken coop drinking his
eggs. How could I stop myself wanting to hear more?
I believed in the pale-skinned women with doe eyes,
Victorian lace at their neck and ankles and nothing else.
I saw them half-hidden in the straw. Pointing their toes
on the roosts like a ballet of droppings. He would wave
his hands around me like a camera panning. It was as if
he guessed one day I'd act, my celebrity ballooning into
Jupiter, gravity and gas, a flaming wandering. The purple
giant. A pharaoh trailed by murdered handmaidens. His
visions I remembered when I played Lilith. One day I

would witness naked women climbing fire escapes or clutching the wheel of my weaving Renault, trying to steal swallows of my gin and Seconal.

*Q: You spoke of your great-uncle's visions in relation to
your roles. In the middle of your career you'll write these
words to a friend: "I went to see Jean Claude in the hospital
and while I was there put on a white uniform and helped
with an open heart surgery." Talk about the hallucinatory
quality of* Lilith, *considered one of your best performances.*

SEBERG: I don't remember writing those words. Who
hasn't read Isaiah? *She shall become an abode for jackals
and a haunt for ostriches.* The Lilith. *Wildcats shall
meet with desert beasts, satyrs shall call to one another;
There shall the lilith repose.* Original sexual predator
and strangler of sleeping men. Bird talons for feet
and a scorpion between her legs, the demi-goddess of
storm, she who suckles dogs and pigs at her milkless
breasts. Hollywood's no Babylonian Talmud. They
keep my Midwestern twang and dress me in prim
cotton. Disguise my boy-hair with a blond wig, then
order me to hunt the fragile lightning bugs, or better
still, lower a bucket into the unexplored self. I'm to
become a temptress, a schizophrenic housed in a
wooded sanitarium let loose at midday to wander. Every
afternoon I'm laughing, but I crave myself most and
slip between the shagbark hickories. There are peaches
swaying in the breeze. Black flies bite like tiny vampire
bats. I wade into the lake slashed by sun and shadow, lift
my skirt above my knees and bend to kiss my reflection.
I'm the girl next door with a viper's twist. Watch my

smile try to hide itself when Peter Fonda, a bespectacled
fellow patient, attempts to drown himself to prove his
love. If I were queen I would serve only apricots and
dates toothpicked through by thistle. I would seduce the
panting peonies, entice the long grass and draw summer
lightning and thunderclap. Not just the caregiver
attendant, Warren Beatty, so young you won't recognize
his boyish innocence raised from its grave. I take him in
my arms. Desolation is where we rent our bed. Between
my breasts there's floating broken ice and frigid water
estuaries. On my near perfect face my lips are quivering
wings of arctic swans. Isaiah 34:14: *and the shrichowle
shall rest there, and shall finde for her selfe a quiet dwelling.*
I sense my great-uncle's vision of tree-climbing soul
nakedness.

Q: Interestingly, you held the record for most books checked out from the Marshalltown Public Library. When the French language's beauty attracted you and wasn't offered in your school, you taught it to yourself. Yet, in movie roles, you played ingénues, frigid housewives, bordello madams, and the bitch-goddess-muse, the schizophrenic Lilith. Did directors have any idea how to use you?

SEBERG: They want an orchid whore so I am cast. Beauty isn't a marzipan cookie, no exotic island of almond paste, not even a meringue's bite of sweet cloud. It gets you in the door. But once there, the scripts they offer are lump crab. Fish skeletons in lingerie carted around on silver platters. They scuff mud from the soles of their boots and call it a role. I stare into the water. A shot. The camera loves me from every angle. I have the rare gift. Some actresses try to smile but their mouth doesn't help them at all. My face is a beautiful room, another camera angle, a mysterious sky. Midshot, my frown's a soft nutmeg leather chair. Tears grow in my eyes like weeds. The taste of blood is from where the close-up bit my tongue. A sidewalk preacher wanders about inside me shouting purple words, "Scourge the wench!" But I say, "Raise the fallen!"

SEBERG: ACCIDENTAL ACTRESS

Q: Bonjour Tristesse, *as directed by Otto Preminger,*
considered a failure at the time, is now hailed as a critical
masterpiece. Of the three lead actors David Niven,
Deborah Kerr and Jean Seberg, your performance is said
to cut deepest. Is this another case of you being a woman
ahead of your time?

SEBERG: As the first modern anti-heroine, I'm
beautiful, yet spookily sinister picking at a string of
pearls. See the jut of my wing bones. Water lilies float
across their pond of shallow water; each stalk has a
secret in its petals. Preminger explains how the root
detaches and sinks itself in new mud at the bottom of
the pond. *Nymphaea Juno* blooms nocturnally. "You are
the night lily," he berates me. "Charming and ruthless.
Remain expressionless." I play Cecilie. An amoral
teenager who tinkers with her bachelor father's love life.
I am possessive of him yet allow him his charm bracelet
mistresses little older than me. The hint is incest but
only a whiff. Preminger liked to watch me bathe. He
believed I was a virgin. Couldn't he see? Your hands can't
come clean once they've handled sex. It's in your skin.
Your fingers. Though once I forced my legs into it. It's
like the scent of death. Try, suicide-girl, to polish the
jagged lip of a can from your wrist. You can't. It leaves a
strong sharpness like limburger. An aftertaste. The lout

boyfriend in the hall. You know the girls who audition
half-naked. They wear mosquitoes on their earlobes like
tiny birds. I smack my arm, interrupt their blood meal.
It's the Place de la Bastille rising.

*Q: Twice you were directed by husbands, Romain Gary
and Dennis Berry, and one cast you as a nymphomaniac
and the other as a madam. Tell us about the movie* Birds in
Peru, *the first to receive the X rating. You were said to have
"hang-ups" about your body, although on the set you and
Romain discussed endlessly your character's perversities.
"There was something distinctly unhealthy about the whole
project," supporting actress Betty Desouches remarked. Do
you agree?*

SEBERG: You be the judge. Gulls and terns and
pelicans come to a certain beach in Peru to die. And no
one knows why. In the film I'm Adrianna who makes a
pact with her husband. If not cured of the sex sickness,
he may kill me. Who would accept a script like that?
An Iowa girl who trusts Romain, my brilliant author
husband? The opening headshot shows a woman's face
pushed rhythmically into the sand. Four fishermen
ravage me on the beach where flocks of birds commit
suicide. You can't see the huge pieces of driftwood,
whole trunks with stubby ashen limbs. Like fucking
a prehistoric forest. I smell the birds. The fish inside
them. Primitive life. I pass out. Wake, tasting fire in
my mouth, yellow amber grape brandy. This is how I'm
showcased. In an agony of heat. Not a long-tailed sylph
or a flamingo but a slit staring bald-eyed at the sun.
   A full shot finds me dancing, radiant, eyelids wearing
a willow shiver, my dress tight. The scene calls for an

adventurer and a condor. When the adventurer shows I
bed him standing up, then run to a bordello and make
girl-love to the madam. Kissing me with her night
breath, and then me needing her again. An extreme long
shot of an overheated sunset, bruise-colored clouds,
purple and yellow shot through with red. Parrots watch
from the trees, their lime feathers flowing like green
river phosphate at my father's drug store, and begin to
scream. A critic said in a tight close-up I resemble a
girl about to lose a spelling bee not one in the throes
of emotion. It didn't deserve the rating X, not this
comedy. Yet I understood the stone trunks, their roots
of whitened eels. I knew the condor's visions. His black
eyes' glitter. Judging how my body will at last attract
him. Wedged between the Renault's front and back seat.
Fully nude and for eleven days decomposing.

Q: Friends say part of your problem was marrying Frenchmen. Talk about returning to Marshalltown, after making Saint Joan *and* Bonjour Tristesse *to marry twenty-three-year-old François Moreuil, an aspiring film director. "François was an overgrown French version of a fraternity boy," you would tell a reporter. "He had a compulsion to socialize every night at any Whiskey a Go-Go jukebox."*

SEBERG: François preferred all-night St. Tropez and for our wedding insisted upon caviar throned in silver bowls and roasted turkey deboned, then reassembled. I brought him to great-uncle Billy's for Sunday meal. I was 20, he 24. A Lutheran lull cast itself over the sexless grass, gray-shingled and fenceless; the leghorns and pilgrim red rocks scratched the warm dirt for bugs. Eggs were once the hard currency of this world. François shivered, wondering what the earthworm felt fished from its eyeless deep into the yellow, chipped beak. "Worm," I laughed wildly, pecking him with my nose. I'd forget how the sweetness of my teasing bubbled in my throat. The barn's Dutch doors padlocked long dead sinners in, a boy and girl lying fully-fleshed in a splintery maze of hay. I'd seen their apparitions as a child. I showed him to the outhouse where sun fought through the ruined roof. Take your pick. Cobs for tissue or chamois-soft catalogue pages of Sears' refrigerators. Wasps buzzed in the far reach eaves. I scatted one with

my hand. Two hole seats here. Bride and groom. Sit,
Monsieur Cosmopolitan. I kissed the black banquette
of his mustache. Then I sat. His mystifying wife. You
could hear the sound of pee falling to the bottom like a
suicide's leap, the breeze that carried refrains of clucking.

Q: Marshalltown certainly didn't understand New Wave filmmaking, a very different technique from Hollywood. They accused you of being "Europeanized." That the actress they saw on-screen was the off-screen life.

SEBERG: In *Bonjour Tristesse* they painted me as the accidental actress. Critics savaged me. Here on-screen (*Le Grand Delire*) I'm in a tawdry hotel room with a young Frenchman. The music is sulky-mouth jazz. We become lovers, and then he confesses that he is only sixteen. I pout behind a wisp of cigarette smoke. If I'd listened to Marshalltown I'd be like my mother tinting my hair to excite myself. Chestnut, red/bronze, twin colors of blood and shield hammered together. I'd wear an amber ring to delight an infant's innocent eye. Happily snug, I'd never yearn. Watch me collect bits of loveliness. Lick the ruby water of a child's cut finger, polish glass fruits in a wooden bowl. I'd call it enough admiring grapes that never age or shining apples with their ripeness painted on. I'd serve Velveeta Cheese and Jiffy biscuits. Jello salad. In the stillness I would search out the smell of trees between my legs.

Q: Of your three husbands, François was the one you married in a church. Soon you'd call the newlyweds in their picture frame an abandoned house, not even the fireplace standing. Your affection for him ephemeral and fading faster than the smell of his shaving cream. Why wed in such a highly publicized setting when you would shortly accuse him of mental cruelty and discard him?

SEBERG: I married in church to please my past. His very black hair and skin the white of sanctuary air, made me pale beside him. A tulle gown breeds the heavy scent of peonies, a solemn grave heaped over vows. Why should I complain? I'm every Iowa girl's dream of fame. I'm not smothering under the veil my forebears sprang from—Irish Potato Famine refugees and Swedes who roped reins around their waists and drew the plow. A wedding is a stomach rumbling through its black tuxedo. TV cameras panning. A photographer's flash that heaves its flat iron through glass. A rustiness the honeymoon seeps from. François was a boy with big emotions. Ask, he'll tell you how dearly he paid for them. I was already divorcing him as they pronounced us man and wife.

Q: François insisted you accompany him to a dinner at the French Embassy. You expected a stiff, awkward evening; the host, the French consul-general, almost your father's age. And there was Romain Gary: sophisticated, freely speaking of his critically acclaimed novels, his physique a fighter pilot's. A year later you auditioned for In the French Style. *You were pregnant at the time with your still-married lover's child. How did you win both the part and Romain's divorce from the writer Leslie Branch?*

SEBERG: I listen to Diego's every kick inside me, his tossing and turning, how the current in a river must sleep. My belly makes sounds like a washing machine when the towels and sheets twist together and throw the balance off. I want chokecherries at midnight, sour and tart. In Barcelona they come to the hospital to audition me for the role of Christina, the art student ingénue. I am in the last months of pregnancy, ballooning, recently divorced from François and carrying Romain's child. All of this I've kept hidden from the press. I pretend I've broken my leg and Romain fashions an arch over it. Months pass before shooting starts and by then I've even lost my baby fat. In *In the French Style* the girl I play is me. Expatriate, on the run, discovering men. I lift Romain's right hand to my lips, kissing his knuckles, sniffing traces of his orange blossom scent. If he doesn't marry me I'll die, I think, after endless months of his wife's indecision. A Russian Tatar, his

Mongolian eyes are the cloudless blue of famine and
boiling stallion. Born in Lithuania, his Jewish mother
stole away with him to Nice. My father's age, he flew
for DeGaulle's Free French. He calls me *Naiad*. Water
nymph or aquatic insect. I've never heard the word
pronounced in a human mouth. Diego will inherit those
wild stallion eyes. By the time our son reaches age 16,
Romain and I are gone, a year apart by suicide.

SEBERG: DIEGO'S MOTHER

Q: It's 1962 and the birth of your son Alexandre Diego seems shrouded in mystery. After meeting you on a movie set, Joanne Woodward is quoted as saying, "Jean would talk very strangely about this child she had, a child of hers and Romain's. I never quite understood it. They'd sent it away or put it out in the country." Why did you allow your middle-aged Spanish maid Eugenia Munoz to raise Diego in Barcelona? He learned Spanish as his first language. For visits your son was brought to Paris. What did he consider home?

SEBERG: Eugenia's kitchen. Tick tock, the drip of quiet minutes, the hissing of the kettle about to steep tea. A peeled egg, pristine and white, rests on the countertop in its innocence. Diego, little owl, with his father's Asiatic blue eyes on the pure flame of his face, is born wise. At seven he tells me in Spanish mixed with French about how the sky's shyness reminds him of a deer. *Venado.* Red deer. He holds his fist to his forehead. *Asta.* Antler. He plays in the patio sun feeling it torch the black of his hair. How safe he is with Eugenia, her colorful skin like clay or rain on rust, like snow brushed off a rake bearded with dirt. That is the fragrance of red skin. Big as a giant anteater, she gardens the food eaten here, and as they weed Diego talks to the squash's curling yellow vines, to the swimming white blossoms. Ten corn ears steadied by silk to their stalks are his. I clap and cover him in kisses. It is his praise talk, not only rain and sun that coaxes green from soil. Once I saw a fawn that'd lost its mother swim the Iowa River in flood. The fawn reached the opposite bank and stumbled up, bewildered, vulnerable. Better my son has more mothers than one.

Q: Help us understand why Diego ultimately had two mothers—his surrogate mother and you. Outwardly, two women could not have looked more unalike—Eugenia, overweight, suffering from phlebitis in her legs; and you, a beautiful film star. Is it true that when you tried to pry him away from her he would throw savage tantrums?

SEBERG: These questions all seem headed in the same direction—wanting me to paint myself a bad mother, to admit regret. In Barcelona Picasso painted the Catalan Coast with smudged brushstrokes—sky, water, and buildings a blurry blue—except for a donkey pulling a cart. Ask Picasso why he was a donkey toward his little son Paolo, to belittle then disown him. Eugenia instructs Diego about boiled eggs. Let them cool in the palms of your hands, and then run water over them. My son picks bits of brown shell from the white, and asks where the chick is. How can I eat this? Will it be like swallowing myself? *Cervato*, she calls him. Fawn. *Buho*. Tiny owl. Eugenia takes him to mass and tells me her *Cervato* cups his ears and listens to the jackdaws roosting in the old church rafters, their feathers the color of incense. Her *Buho* finds their songs pleasing as do the ears of Christ nailed to his timber. When nocturnal dream-birds screech he climbs into Eugenia's bed. Only she can protect him from the night bird's tin can talons and flypaper wings that little boys stick to. Understand me, Diego, I could only be your sometimes mother. I could call you painted frog, fill your playroom with riverbanks and snails. I felt you already capable of anything. A career is a solar storm, a little god, magnetic field, flares, the radiance that hurtles your white-hot frozen bits into an asteroid belt. But I loved you and you knew it. Yes, I filmed *In the French Style* two weeks after your birth; yes, I handed you over to an aging nursemaid. I played the part of a student, a flirting virgin. I had no choice.

*Q: Each year you made your annual pilgrimage home.
After your separation from Romain you took Diego with
you to Iowa. You wanted him to meet his grandparents and
experience the wonders of a small town in July. How was
that first meeting between your parents and your son?*

SEBERG: I want to show Diego everything. The fields'
deep cellars that remember the seven-foot prairie
grasses swooning as they burned, that sought the sun
and were cut down. Earth can't forget the six-yoked
oxen in their wedding trains of harnesses, dig digging
furrows with iron plows. You can still lie down with
the seed, wrap the black soil like sable around you,
and be resurrected. Diego plays with his cousins using
children's sign language, but with his grandparents he
falls silent. Goldfinches no bigger than pinkie fingers
are singing near the back step. He hears the pansies
whispering. At their centers are blotches in the shape
of butterflies, each a mystery where Pandora lives. A
cloudburst sends us in to supper. Seated at the white
edge of a table cloth, my son picks the blood trickle of
a red embroidery thread. His grandparents, tall eyelash
trees, look down in awe. To them this beautiful exotic
boy might as well be mute. They can't understand a
word he says in Spanish or French unless I translate.
At the window fireflies spark their tiny flashlights,
caressing the night as it gently boils.

SEBERG: BLACK PANTHER

*Q: In the late '60s and early '70s you began to immerse
yourself in radical politics. In LA you rented the Coldwater
Canyon house that soon became a late night stop for Black
Panthers. Romain and Diego visited, and then returned
to Paris. How did you merge activism and intimacy with
certain party members?*

SEBERG: I hate injustice like the Los Angeles smog. I
watch Jamal unwrap a .22-caliber pistol from a baggie
and load five bullets. We huddle at the table's middle
within reach of the candlelight, our heads bent. The
chandelier sheds light through Jamal's goblet, wine
pooling in the wood grain's open mouths. The Panthers
are arming themselves in Oakland, they follow police
cars about to make arrests. They're carrying shotguns
in Watts. A gutted sun, gin-colored, shines on the old
riot ground. When I look at him the waves of anger
strike me, his cougar-teeth bite through my eyelids. The
vessels in my brain constrict—I want to hit the walls,
tear apart a window shard by shard. Angry at anything
that constrains, restricts. Last word, authority of any
kind. I want to scrape off the wool blanket of my pale
skin. I am a white panther, the pale variant that Romain
sends flowers to from Paris—frayed petals that scatter
over the carpet or maybe it's a moth with gold-dusted
wings that has been stepped on. My husband has

nothing but scorn for Hollywood liberals. "You may need this," Jamal says, "if my wife comes to visit." The pistol lies on the table between us. There is quiet and what little noise the maid Celia makes the willow carpet absorbs. Night breezes carry smoke rising from a ditch, the peculiar scent of earth and fire and billyclubs. We speak of constitutional rights and school lunch vouchers for the needy. His voice a melting humidity, his mouth has enjoyed the ladies' sweet marmalade but his eyes have slaughtered. "A woman wet smells like musky leaves and sardines," he says, carrying me upstairs. I start Operation Love.

*Q: Your Panther period was a volatile atmosphere of
jealous wives, mock shootouts, and poisoned cats.* You
rented cars, provided food and sex, and hid guns. After
you were targeted by Cointelpro as a radical sympathizer,
the FBI kept you under surveillance. And you mention
wiretapping. What was it like?*

SEBERG: They're listening. A radio alarm is blinking.
A noise that chants Bible verses and translates into
Chinese. *Anyone who does not love his brother, whom
he has seen, cannot love God, whom he has not seen.*
In my kitchen I make circles with my feet to throw
them off my trail. I flint blades from blue stone.
COINTELPRO. Wiretaps make it difficult. I grind
my heel into the carpet rather than chat. They're
everywhere. Hunched in vans. In my refrigerator. The
sky's a legion of wiretapping men in suits and ties with
close-cropped hair. I hear them mutter. *Jean Seberg must
be neutralized. The promiscuous wench.* J. Edgar Hoover
prances through my dreams in a black satin off-the-
shoulder dress and a string of long white pearls. *How
would she like an FBI .38 shoved into her?* My crime a
$12,000 contribution for an inner-city soup kitchen. The
migraines come. I darken my bedroom to full night. The
surveillance team has set up a volleyball net in the flat
above. Wrist bones spank the ball like claps of thunder.
The concierge tells me no one lives up there. Yet day and
night I decipher planted messages.

Nembutals soften the hook they've pierced me with.
My soul's hiding under a fish rag.
While the white trout moon suckles all of Paris, I
nurse on my pillow.

* [*You say the FBI poisoned them. Romain Gary believes it
was a Panther wife.*]

Q: The FBI called you a degenerate-idealist, a mark. They tracked who you slipped checks to, not only your friends and family, but groups like school lunch programs for inner city children, and they'd learned you'd set up your Vietnamese make-up artist in her own flower shop and suspected it was a front. But your interracial love affairs were said to be the real triggers for the FBI. On May 1, 1973, your friend Hakim Jamal, a black activist, was murdered. How did his death affect you?

SEBERG: I stood in a tee-shirt and white skirt and leaned over the railing, then I stepped back and pulled my skirt up, fanning my slip and legs as if airing myself. I bit back my breath. Jamal thought he was the Almighty. He wanted to speak for the cosmos. To free us all from slavery. He liked to lay his women on two folding chairs, head on one, feet on the other, and by his consciousness cause their bodies to vibrate, and then levitate. Your soul might be breaking from snow's weight, but when he spoke it flowered into a pale orange monarch.

That's what his voice was. Inside his eyes the forests of Mexico waited, high altitude humid ones where butterflies migrated.

I flew a continent to him. Stupid.

Thousands of silken soft wings ricocheting between treetops until a million fluttered. He gestured and my torso rose. Could I doubt him? An English heiress

introduced us. It was pure belief. Sometimes he applied
the blindfold. Who can't remember the dark of one
monarch trembling on your skin then hundreds seeking
warmth in your body's crevices, sounding like a great
sob. You are the tree and your arm-branches flood.
Afterwards you write checks. More and more checks
until you realize you've been duped. The weight of that
more crushing than a wall, a living weight in pieces—
the gilt silkiness shorn by amber wings. A con man's
cocoon. I suffocated standing up. The night four killers
buzzed his door, he let them in. They were friends who
put bullets through his temple. They left him wearing
a leather thong that cupped his groin like old coins in a
Rome fountain. A huckster's death. Still I wept.

Q: In 1970 the FBI planted the false story that you were pregnant not by your husband but by a member of the Black Panther Party. The story's purpose was to "cheapen your image." Subsequently, you took an overdose of barbiturates. Why?

SEBERG: You know why, don't you? They called me the last all-American girl and so I could never forsake the Midwest. How could I shame Marshalltown? My watching parents? My first child Diego floated out of me in a dark house in Spain, an old lantern room that once burned a thicket of candles in a revolving chandelier. His father, Romain Gary, believed we made love best in noonday sun. No one could accuse me of frigidity. Still, I refused to do nudity on-screen. Pregnant with my second child, the *LA Times* broke the Black Panther story.* A gift in fuchsia and lavender. Bees buzzed above me like a trance. I followed a trail of butterfly corpses leading me to a water lily world. I overdosed and accidentally lived, but two days later my baby died.

Nina, darling, my white-coffin baby. Forgive me, my barbiturate infant.

The lily forest swamped me. My feet sank in muck and I couldn't free them. I became psychotic or so said Romain, but how can you trust the word of a novelist? Everyone knows about the silences that must be filled.

* Privately, I'd slept with two Panther men but not anywhere near the conception. The *LA Times* story was factually untrue.

Q: Pretend your father still owns Seberg Drug Store where he grinds potions to powder with mortar and pestle. There's the quiet air, the cash register with its wooden drawers, and the soda counter's blaze of ice cream meeting the molten hot fudge. If you could redo one event of your life and relive it with a different outcome, what would it be?

SEBERG: If God would allow it I'd give birth to my daughter again. Once I dreamed it real. My first two husbands are the midwives and I'm back in Iowa at my great-uncle's. The orchard. I'm lying between apple trees and filling my lungs with the cider perfume of the cool ground. Romain is feeling my belly to see if the baby has fallen down. Above me black grapes tug their wiry vines. Francois elevates my pelvis. Back arched, my mouth's a croak. I rake my fingers into earth. Romain smears fresh butter on my stomach and between my legs softening my uterus, touching, widening the place for the baby. Francois wetting my face. *Don't look too hard at the ceiling. The girl will never grow breasts. Don't stare at the black green leaves or the child will be full of envy. Moon watching creates a sleepwalker.* Pushing, the legs propped, the hardest work. My head singing with dusk mourning doves. Romain's hands catch the sluice, fingers there to cradle the girl-thing sliding into this world. Jelly-being, creature fresh from infinity, held up by her feet, crying. I'll blanket us both in ground-soaking summer rain. The cord cut. Test the baby girl's cry, count her toes. I make her breathe.

SEBERG: ON LOCATION

Q: What does it mean to be on location?

SEBERG: You immolate your brain in a haze of golden
tequila and forget the dirty heat blistering your feet.
Your other selves no longer exist. Home is the faraway
place. You dress in the blonde skin of a beast and learn
all the rhumba steps, so it's a vacation with the camera's
great whitening eye staring you down. For Morocco
and Mexico I packed a lavish ooze of coconut oil and
unraveling bikini straps. I added my Hemingway reader.
There you are on a desert island with only the cast
and crew for family. Once we shot in a village outside
Mexico City. They set up food tables for us. Skinny
dogs, their huge eyes like mouths, loped over. I fed them
from my plate. "Oh, you don't do that in this country," I
was chastised, "not when people are going hungry." My
fork froze. "Dogs are better people than most I know,"
I said, choking. Location is a heated air where you can
breathe only the smoldering between co-stars. A crush
hooks you like an amberjack, broils you on wood chips,
and burns your marriage down. Hot was Madrid, then
Alicante on the Costa Brava, and hotter still, Tunisia.
Hottest was Paint Your Wagon, the silliest musical
since none of the stars could sing a note. Skinny dogs
sheltering between mesquite trees find their way into
my sleep. Through it all I hear their whimpering. The

long shot reels you in for the close-up. You have no
family, no past. No son, no husband. You're whatever
the script asks. Lily or green toad.

Q: Paint Your Wagon (1969) is set in Gold Rush era California. For your love scenes you insist on a body stocking. How do we reconcile that with the image of a "sexually insatiable woman,"—words used to describe you? Do you blame being on location for the affair with your co-star and the breakup of your second marriage?

SEBERG: His gaze lands its sand fly on your thigh, a sting before waves break over the buttocks of the beach. C.E.* was terribly handsome. Location seduces you and the gray glaze you stare at. There's the strong smell of bodies, the he-man whose scent is curry and musk. C.E., the kind of man who does his own dishes, a real American my grandmother would approve of. Not like the Frenchmen I married. But leading man love is a chimera, the transitory nature of a movie being made. It's the dark marsupial flesh of a border town, men wanting to get lost in its red mouth. C.E. couldn't stay away. He settled over me in a pool of crude oil. Back on Paramount's Hollywood lot, my co-star cut me dead. Divorce ahead, venting impurities and green flames to the sky, the horizon on fire. You go it alone.

* [C.E. aka Clint Eastwood]

Q: While working on Macho Callahan *in Mexico City
you met the celebrated writer Carlos Fuentes and had a
two-week affair. Afterwards, he wrote the novel* Diana
*about you. Because of your blend of intelligence, kindness,
and beauty, ["Jean's was a sweet face where hate didn't
easily find a home," wrote Romain Gary] writers seem
especially enthralled by you. What were your impressions?*

SEBERG: The sun beats down on Juarez; a fickle bell
tolls. In Durango as in Morocco, air is territory. A house
is dying for a breeze, and a lipsticked actress passes out,
her flimsy clothes sweated and heavy, make-up melting
on her face. It's a flat-bed truck bringing your co-star
and squares of sod. You live on a diet of calamari and
margaritas with hard-salted lips. Location is paradise.
It's hell. Azaleas burst their blooms. Corpus Christi bay,
the thorny body of Christos, the glistening bay blues
the horizon; the white sand throws its grain toward the
seawall. But on the brown-skinned side of town, low
stucco houses lurch toward the refineries. You eat thorns
if the scripts tell you to do it. Location is a stranger
taking your sun-drenched breast in his mouth and your
nipple not objecting. What's real is make-believe. You're
inoculated against the mundane. The sky is Mustang
Island where horses are pulling the wind with sand-
crusted nostrils. And sheephead fish smoke on ice.
You're turning blue, you're the last oxygen, you're a body
used up. Carlos considered me intelligent and cultured,
nothing infantile about me. Nice to oil a fingertip and
slide it over an unexplored shoulder.

Q: In 1964 you play a seductive schizophrenic who engineers the suicide of another patient. Your performance received a Golden Globe nomination for Best Actress Drama. In 1971, you accepted the starring role in Nelo Risi's The Dead of Summer. *Was it difficult filming when you again play a schizophrenic woman who is dogged by visions of having killed her husband?*

SEBERG: Shot in Agadir, Morocco, a seaside city an earthquake leveled years before, the script is tormented by heat and sand. Arab boys swarm over my car. I get out and nearly faint in the sun. I conjure snow, the trapped space between crystalline flakes. Haunted by waking dreams of having killed my husband (a German architect), I walk endlessly through the streets. Sunfish with needle-like teeth glint from shop windows. I envision my hand with a blade in it. My breath moves in and out, fast. I can't see my husband, only my breath. He falls, clutching the air. Sky. A copper sun beaten into the horizon. I scrape the scales from a fisherman's knife and press them into my skin made sticky by the wind. You can drown in the little ocean inside. A stranger offers me a sea snake wrapped in a newspaper. A language of desert where water has crept. I hear the humming of the eel-like being. A gold fin runs the length of its blue ribbon body. A mane on its head rises into a magnificent crest as if a goddess had been punished for her murderousness. My performance was praised.

Q: *We associate you with Paris, so why in your directorial debut did you pick an American icon like Billy the Kid for subject matter? "I am 35 and have spent half my life walking back and forth in front of a camera," you wrote in a letter home. "It's strange for a woman to see her face and very being change." How does Star, the has-been actress who crosses paths with Billy, reflect those changes in your inner being?*

SEBERG: I act, direct, and produce the last meeting of the last two people in the world. Billy the Kid meets Star, the washed-up film goddess. The Kid wears flip-flops and a ripped shirt. A French accent masks a western twang. He's waiting there in the trees. Watching the dying world's moon wax and wane in the pool, he stirs the spirant ashes. This is the hour of the mockingbird, of black and white plumage. The six-shooter. Tell me this isn't the magic of cinema. I play God and return Billy the Kid to this earth. He's just been shot, gasped out his last words in Spanish. His corpse stolen and promenaded across the desert west. Dark-haired, lithe as a filament wire, he's an orphan before he steps into legend. A self-cocking revolver who kills his first man at 18. Billy's skin is rice-water pale. Call his eyes twilight or bluish smoke, he's pacing through the chaise lounges, his finger twitching. He tells you about territories where the Apaches fight to the last bloody cactus. He rinses his teeth, spits, and calls it a bath. His pulse shivers, his soul's a tepid blur. Where else you can you make this happen? Give a has-been a second chance.

Q: You once said, "So much of acting is good luck that it's quite unfair and unjust." Any advice for an aspiring actress like me wanting to follow in your footsteps?

SEBERG: How badly do you want it? They'll tell you LA is the capital of the universe. Only Hollywood is cosmopolitan. And if you prove to them they aren't world class, they'll hate your guts. You think that fame is an escape from the sidewalk and entrée to the limo that rides you to private afterhours where the saxophone player sweats in a suit of blue ostrich feathers and the trumpet player is high on nitrous oxide. You arrive on the arm of an aging fill-in-the-blank *[i.e., director, actor, screenwriter, agent, publicist]*. You sip apricot brandy and lick maraschino cherries. You're willing to be speared by red plastic, and you're tagged a swashbuckler, the perk ordered up by the club. Soon you're a porcelain bowl, offering yourself like a chilled plum. The call girl is usually shorter than the leggy one who breathes the higher altitudes, and that's how you know the difference between a girlfriend and a model, between a prostitute and an actress. It's all about height. The back room is where the important stuff happens. A leather curtain scorched by the grief of armadillos divides the audience from the action. When you're an aspiring anything you learn to wait with the buffet table, a feast of purple grapes and serpent-green kiwi. Back rooms are black

as the water in Navigation Channel. Look out for oil
tankers coming in from Qatar. Don't become an actress
expecting the public to love you like your grandfather
did your grandmother. That takes singing in the church
choir. That calls for purity. He, fifteen and she, twelve.
You're not the only girl whose succulence is salable, who
is waiting for the chance to be burned at the stake.

SEBERG: EXPAT

Q: It's 1956 and you spend your first June after high school performing in summer stock. You're given the local beauty queen's role in Picnic—*William Inge's play about a Kansas backwater. There's a moment when the daily train passes and the characters hear the faraway whistle. They stop and listen. Talk about that moment.*

SEBERG: Forty of us, young actors and actresses from the city, except for me from a small town. They can't understand the train whistle. I tell them in a backwater town that whistle means escape. If you come from the same everyday lunch sack of rye bread and molasses-smear the sound explodes in your soul. It's a boy looking at you with beautiful hazel eyes. The field you lie down in when he kisses you and holds your face in his hands. His breath in your mouth and yours in his. It's a taffeta girl in the shape of an hourglass. A distant country mapped in pale tangerine. A huge amber ring that can sing. If you live in a place of weeds and dust and six months of winter, it's a lust for the equatorial sun. A long-limbed nakedness. The drayhorse lady of the house faces Monday, cleaning; Tuesday, bread-making; Wednesday, washing; then the whistle is a bride and groom of 19 making their getaway. The whistle means breakout. Live. Wear heat lightning for your wedding dress. And the green swaying from the

branches is your bouquet to throw away. All aboard.
Not one townsperson makes a move. No one ever does.
One day I'll be called lightning in a bottle. One day I'll
run naked on a plane from the bathroom to first class.
International flights carry you only so far. It's the falling,
the getting up on hands and knees, the crawling that my
fellow actors can't understand.

*Q: You lived most of your adult life in Paris, yet a
friend said, "I don't think she ever really got away from
Marshalltown." I'm curious whether you would compare
yourself to Josephine Baker, another ex-pat, with her
cheetah-on-a-leash and internationally famous banana
dance pole-vaulting her from St Louis's illegitimate
daughter to French citizenship and full military honors at
her funeral?*

SEBERG: Like Baker I pleased Paris but I could not
please Marshalltown. Back home only the animals
and trees believe in truth. The birds stay honest. Wet
feathers, manure: smells the melting ground gives
up are real. My grandmother Frances Bensen (G.G.)
spoke of her school days' potbelly stove only heating a
quarter of the room. Two long tables, a board to write
on with charcoal and sharpened stick. No one believes
I used to wash G.G.'s feet. "You'll dirty your hands," she
warned. I was fascinated by the indigo veins around her
ankles—blue roots keeping her trunk upright. Being a
novice actress under the tyrant Preminger made me cold
as the one-room school, but he wanted me hot. "Who
do you think you are, Sir John Gielgud? You'll wear
what I say." Today it's long underwear and clunky boots,
coarse things with drawstrings and buttons. "You're no
actress, you're a ham." Tomorrow he'll have me imagine
myself—dirty bathwater, nothing's tooth and tongue,
barnyard goose. He was another I could not please.

Morality in the Midwest keeps the skies grey; the snow, a black stone; the moon a torn piece of bread; and sex layers deep under the homespun dress. I stole my sister's boyfriends, but not intentionally. That, too, was in me. Salt. Blood. Gut. Sex here is the grit of cracked pepper on the body of a chicken. Tears. A perfumed mustiness. Grandmother Bensen kept a detailed diary in formal script in her safety deposit box. I made a diary on my body. A London film critic wrote about my Saint Joan. "What miscasting! Seberg never discards her decorative niceness and her emotional range is that of a debutante at an awkward party." How I proved him wrong. I self-mutilated, my nightgown pulled up, legs covered by bruises. An awful Puritanism.

Q: Otto Preminger made you famous overnight in Saint
Joan, *and then destroyed any confidence you might have
had in yourself as an actress. Would you consider that a
true statement?*

SEBERG: It's true and you know that. For the audition
he sits on a raised platform, (like a grand pigeon
throned in an air shaft) his face a spotlight. I don't wear
a cross like the rest. I go in ballet slippers. I go in bare
feet. Preminger wants me and four others—a Swede,
Russian, Brit, another American—for a final audition.
My druggist father balks. "Ve do not gobble little girls
in New York," Otto says and takes another bite of his
fat red apple. When I win he orders my hair cut. Beauty
marks scoured. The heat, you can't imagine all the heat
in 28 pounds of armor. His yelling in my face. "You're
a phony Joan of Arc." Like the critic who'll echo, "Saint
Joan was a crust of black bread soaked in blood and red
wine, Seberg is a honeybun." Yet I captivate the great
director. Every morning his fresh violets appear in my
dressing room. When I'm accused and brought before
the Inquisition, his hyena breath melts the makeup on
my face. "You're not thinking the part!" Twenty takes.
Like a pot thrown on a stove, the water boiled out, and
now it's the pan roiling. The tyrant is still shouting,
"You're not thinking the part. Break!" I break. I sob
hysterically while Otto strokes my head and murmurs,
"Baby, baby." I am his newborn. The segment of blood

orange he's been slipping through his fingers. Why does he insist on believing me a virgin? Clay. Mud. I think he's a dour stone fish who won't be fooled for his lunch by something dead; he'll feed on what is living or go hungry. He'll shape me; no, he'll create me. A virgin is pure religion. Kerosene. Softness, kinder than fluorescent light, a virgin is tallow, mist surrounds her milky pear breasts. The biggest scene he saves for last. Dragged, I'm manacled to the stake. "Burn her. Burn her." Hooded executioners light the pyre. Five gas cylinders ignite, two explode. Real flames. I scream. Balls of fire lick upward over my stomach, torch my costume. I'm not afraid as Otto's eyes glow red as fire fish. I'm deep in the sky. Alive.

Q: Les Hautes Solitudes (The Outer Reaches of Solitude) *directed by Philippe Garrel. Said to live in a "garret with a rickety table and thousands of cigarette butts." He wanted to make a movie on the "topic of solitude with actors he judged authentically lonely." The silent film became a one-woman Jean Seberg show. Talk about solitude. Its improvised quality.*

SEBERG: The film's an impenetrable 80 minutes of black and white. Single shot close-ups. I drift through empty rooms. My lips move, I comb my fingers with my hair. I touch my face to windows, no outside looks in. It surprises me that I am thirty-four. Garrel sees I can't relax, can't sit still. I hear the fields on either side of me: a badger and civet cat brawling in the brush, a barn owl and timber wolf, cloven hooves. By decade's end I'll be dead. Solitude is hard. Made of spider silk and stronger than steel at its size, yet lightweight. What is authentically lonely? Cold dirt. Orchids' frail white like frozen solid goose down. Winter birds. The sun plucked off beautiful barren trees.

*

SEBERG: Solitude is a 17-year-locust. The nymphs nurse by the thousands on a single tree root. Listen to their chirr and hum. Their life spent underground except for one day in the sun. My career that always just happened has stopped. Alone, I wander into the vestigial eye in the center of my brain, the place where the soul enters and leaves the flesh. I'm among the starving monarch butterflies, those whose tongues cannot close into a straw to sip nectar with, the ragged ones unable to feed. Wearing pale wings, I walk in blanketing snow—the trapped air between singular crystalline flakes. Dusk congeals in white weeds and milkweed tufts.

*

SEBERG: Two thousand kids go missing a day. I once wrote to a Paris newspaper. The kids who disappear in the company of strangers usually never turn up. No begging will change what happens to them. I try to convey that before the camera with my eyes and mouth. Some part of me is already not there. Garrel watches me blow out a candle. Smile. The field gently rolls its hills up to the top of the next rise. I lie in bed where I've become an igloo of sticks and bread wrappers, an upside down nest for a hermit bird. Once I was an explorer. I ambled toward fame, trying to guess what it was and what it was doing in the middle of a field where there wasn't a road.

SEBERG: LATE NIGHT HABITUÉ

Q: Why don't you comment on some of the remarks your friends made about your last year: "At her innermost being, Jean was an incredibly good person. But over the years she had strayed so far from her true nature."

SEBERG: I watch wind stretch me into a long white feather. If the sky's bleak with piled clouds, I smile, and then it blues and yellows and I call it a perfect day. Thrushes and doves fill the leaf breeze of my true nature. The crickets come on with a swoon in my innermost being and the moon rises like clotted butter. The summer world cools. My night sky is seeded with stars the color of field oats. Along the fence line, the innermost Jean can either be caught forever or run. Like house spiders spinning themselves into their own nets, or daddy-long-legs elegantly walking as if the barbed wire is a tightrope stretched above a teeming city street. Understand me. After I said goodbye to goodness there was no way back.

Q: You met Dennis Berry, a struggling film maker, at a Paris discotheque, and married him three weeks later. Son of film director John Berry, blacklisted during the McCarthy era, and penniless, your biographer wrote that you called him a "combination of Harpo and Karl Marx." Was it love?

SEBERG: Dennis calms me. Romain, my second husband, whose name evokes a Caesar salad, appraised my third husband, six years my junior and American, as a worthless acquisition. Dennis's unruly hair possesses the odor of dates and figs hijacked from a velvet-lined buffet. My former husband claimed an intellectual's mustiness, a twelve-place setting's sterling silver. For him I tried *Heart of Darkness* and *Nana*. Spoons too precious to slide against the tongue. Dennis, my film chat, my 4:00 a.m. snack. Dennis, my scriptwriter. My Louvre. With him I tumble down to Levi waistband where my tee-shirt ties in a midriff knot. Yes, I pick up the check. Why not? I'd abandoned Romain's uptight armoire that latched with brass. I chose Dennis's best long-sleeved flannel shirt with top three buttons left undone to walk down the aisle in. I charged the wedding on my credit card. And Paris never forgave me for ditching an ex-consul general Frenchman. Paris can be a tall blond bitch, an Arc de Triomphe iceberg. Paris, all allure in a flaming red sweater, can serve up poisonous scallops and drizzled spinach on crème brûlée. Merci.

*

SEBERG: Three years later I am having a breakdown
and dry heaving the invisible sounds a white trout
makes out of water. I check into a sanitarium, Villa
Montsouris where I crawl toward the wall babbling. I'm
fat. Antidepressants add fifty pounds to me. I will drag
Dennis underwater. I need the arms of a meatier sea
elephant. The fish encyclopedia calls them gentle giants.
At a shark's approach, the depths have seen them fold
divers in their enormous fins. Dennis, my angelic little
sea elephant, has tired of me. Freed for the descent, I
paint my toenails and smoke endless cigarettes.

*Q: You told your mother-in-law a year before your death,
"I used to be a little princess. They'd come and get me in
black limousines. They don't come anymore." You held
court in Paris dives, still a star among the drug addicts and
alcoholics. Talk about that experience.*

SEBERG: Actresses and spiders will eat themselves.
Golden silk spiders [re: producers] look for beautiful
prey and maximum location. Goliath spiders capture
each other in their sleep. Limousines don't come for
turquoise robes pebbled with corn muffin crumbs. I
haven't bathed today. I'll have two goblets filled with red
vodka slush topped with ripe strawberries and plastic
swords. Princesses exist for the eye's delight. They don't
think black thoughts. Will I come back if I leave by my
own hand? People still disappear in parks. My second
husband said, "The saddest of all the exes is the ex-star."
After my last collapse I shoplifted a soot-colored sheath
from a boutique. I could smell my younger body in it.
Don't you see? It had always belonged to me: it wasn't
stealing. In the changing room I noticed a roach, one,
alone. I thought of my critics. The first, the boldest, the
meanest. *Seberg, The Talentless.* It was him scuttling up
the door. I chased him with a piece of dusty Kleenex,
but let him live.

*Q: "Jean desperately needed to feel desired and beautiful,"
said one of your doctors, "when she got fat or developed
dark circles or took on that haggard look, it bothered her
terribly. It was very important for her to feel, well, excuse
the word, 'fuckable.'" Is there any truth to that statement?*

SEBERG: Yes, I sleep on bar floors with my pals. Yes,
my friends suspect me of being a nymphomaniac. Art
and life mesh. I take up with a young Moroccan student
outside a liquor store where I'd broken a bottle. Gâteau,
I christen him, meaning Cookie. My bedmates are all
kinds: Algerians, actors, junkies, musicians with eyes
green like the amyris of radiator fuel, songwriters, and
boys trembling as if newborn antelopes. The winds lift
skirts and bind the couples. Who knows of hair algae
courtship? Fighting fish making circles around their
partners, wild metallic-blue-tipped beings: they literally
explode. Glassfish. Transparent with the iridescent
organs visible. Tiny black dot cocks. Weedy river lice,
kelp beds, clams, oysters. Fish sex is delicious. I've
arrived. I no longer see who is a Mister Magoo, who
has money. Any jazz musician or abstract painter will
do, plumbers welcome, chefs, my husband's friends.
Whoever honors the vodka bottle. I show off my bones
to anyone. Herr Director coaxes the Iowa creek girl to
set down her basket and show her wares—ears of green
corn, chirr of crickets. Green girl like the husk of a
black walnut that falls, splits, and expels the corrugated
nut. She's put inside a sack, taken to the anvil, and
hammered.

SEBERG: COMEBACK

*Q: At Villa Montsouris, an exclusive Paris sanitarium,
where you'd checked in once again, the doctors there were
unable to diagnose your psychological problems, yet they
found you in terrible physical shape. The more your stature
eroded, the more you made up stories of people you bumped
into. "I have an important rendezvous with Fidel Castro
tomorrow," you told your doctor. How did you feel when
celebrities who once knew you turned their backs on you?*

SEBERG: How dumb do you think I am? I've just
turned 40. Alcohol is digesting my liver and blurring my
eyesight. Beasts tuck themselves away in every orifice
of the long narrow hospital corridors. Old movies
endlessly replayed on the ceiling. Backlit rooms with red
ceilings and panels of deer-men and women cavorting
under blood suns. Ibex-horned males like George
Peppard in *Pendulum*. I take a deep breath and stare,
trying not to see myself in the mirror behind his head.
Red red. I've crawled inside bone marrow or a pulsing
heart. "God, you look edible," Peter Sellers from *The
Mouse that Roared* roars, tearing the garlic naan. Otto
Preminger explains about tandoori ovens. All saints
should be baked in them. I enjoy his broad nose and
prominent nostrils. How different do you think humans
are from animals? I want to know. I breathe in Lee
Marvin's eggplant platter, the balsamic rice like a white

breast made of shellacked milk glands. With his index finger he flicks rice from the glass-topped table, and tells me how lions kill the she-lion's offspring to bring her more quickly into heat. The shrinks write on my charts, "All in her head. She's faking it."

Q: In Barcelona at the Music Palace, there are sculptures of women playing instruments, half their bodies coming out of the wall. The tall chimney towers are called scare-witches. In the last week of your life you felt yourself becoming a scare-witch. What was it really like in the backseat of the Renault?

SEBERG: How the hell would I know more than you? I'm murdering both of us. Good girl and bad. I imagine Joan of Arc, her eyes burning, her will, the taste of French in my mouth, éclairs, her knuckles. A sinner, I want the green wind to hear into me, to take ear licks, to scour me clean. My young self taunts the older self with pieces of her body—a spine with bikini straps unraveling, the cleft of a breast. She's smirking while I swallow sleeping pills. "I was magic," she says. "A superb person. Very generous. You betrayed me. You're a drunk who abandoned her own son." I press a pen to the back of an envelope. *Diego, Forgive me. I can no longer live with my nerves. Understand me. I know that you can and you know that I love you. Be strong. Your loving mother, Jean.* I crawl into the Renault's back seat and pull a blanket over my head. Everything begins to shrink. I'm a tree halved, tongue of rope or bark skin split from trunk. Looking up into the miraculous blackness where no bird flies, I'll tell you about the films I never made. The violence I couldn't express. Mushrooms are sprouting from fallen logs tumbling, comforting the spot where my youngest brother wrecked his car. He speaks from the toadstools and fungus; he gives off a pale silvery shiver. Spinning his white blond hair into almost invisible string, he says he's making a hammock of cobwebs to cradle me in. I see a stone house on a cliff set way up on the highest rocks. Who lives there in the sky house? A beautiful actress? An aging celebrity God?

64

NOTES

Thanks to Kate Braverman's short story, "The Collective Voice of Los Angeles Speaks: Marilyn Monroe" for inspiring me. All direct quotes attributed to Jean Seberg, her friends, husbands, directors, or critics are sourced from the below volumes:

Gary, Romain. *White Dog*. Chicago: The University of Chicago Press, 1970.

McGee, Garry. *Jean Seberg Breathless*. Albany, GA: Bear Manor Media, 2008.

Richards, David. *Played Out: The Jean Seberg Story*. New York: Random House, 1981.

ACKNOWLEDGMENTS

Thanks to the editors of the following magazines where sections of the interview have appeared or will appear:

Amoskeag, Antithesis (Australia), *Great Weather for Media: The Understanding between Foxes and Light, Hotel Amerika, Lit 'n Image, Rhino, Menacing Hedge, Nano Fiction, Stone Highway Review, Skidrow Penthouse, SubTerrain,* and *Thrice Fiction,*

COLOPHON

Text is set in a digital version of Jenson, designed by Robert Slimbach in 1996, and based on the work of punchcutter, printer, and publisher Nicolas Jenson.

The titles are in Futura.

STEPHANIE DICKINSON, raised on an Iowa farm, now lives in New York City. Her novel *Half Girl* and novella *Lust Series* were published by Spuyten Duyvil. Other works include the short story collections *Road of Five Churches* and *Port Authority Orchids*. Her story "A Lynching in Stereoscope" was reprinted in *Best American Nonrequired Reading* and "Dalloway and Lucky Seven" and "Love City" in *New Stories from the South*. An associate editor at *Mudfish*, she also assists Rob Cook in editing *Skidrow Penthouse*.

NEW MICHIGAN PRESS, based in Tucson, Arizona, prints poetry and prose chapbooks, especially work that transcends traditional genre. Together with DIAGRAM, NMP sponsors a yearly chapbook competition.

DIAGRAM, a journal of text, art, and schematic, is published bimonthly at THEDIAGRAM.COM. Periodic print anthologies are available from the New Michigan Press at NEWMICHIGANPRESS.COM/NMP.

CPSIA information can be obtained
at www.ICGtesting.com
Printed in the USA
FFOW04n0423180117
31454FF